NAVIGATING
TWEETS, FEATS,
AND DELETES

Advance Praise for
NAVIGATING TWEETS,
FEATS, AND DELETES

"Deceptively simple yet profoundly important tips on how to succeed in today's digitally disrupted workplace. A smorgasbord of brilliant business insights, written to be consumed in small bites: each is digestible, tweetable, and at the same time complex and practical. I wanted to pause after each and savor the secret to success that it belies."

—Glenn Platt, Ph.D., Professor of Marketing and C. Michael Armstrong Professor of Interactive Media at Miami University

"Rich Moran cuts through all the pablum that is on the web today to show us, with wit and humor, what is important and what works at work."

—Kerry A. Dolan, Assistant Managing Editor, *Forbes*

"Somewhere out there someone is reading this book and saying, 'Why didn't anyone ever tell me that?' Moran has created the 'Unwritten Code of Business Success,' bringing perspective back into the workplace. At the least, should be required reading for every new college graduate."

—Greg Ballard, Senior Vice President of Mobile, Social, and Emerging Platforms at Warner Bros. Interactive Entertainment

"One of my favorite acronyms is VUCA (volatility, uncertainty, complexity and ambiguity). VUCA, multiplied by the speed of change, is our world today. In this book, Rich simplifies the challenges we all face in a VUCA world and provides sanguine advice and guidance that can lead us down a better, more healthy and productive path."

—Mike Dulworth, CEO, Executive Networks, Inc. and the author of *The Connect Effect: Building Strong Personal, Professional and Virtual Networks*

"In *Navigating Tweets Feats and Deletes* Moran 'double clicks' on what matters in the workplace. It's not enough to know what to do, we need to know what NOT to do. We need to know that reheated burritos and the 'Reply All' buttons can kill a career. We need to spread the word about these new and classic workplace lessons."

—Stuart Kaplan, President USA, Knightsbridge Human Capital

NAVIGATING TWEETS, FEATS, AND DELETES

Lessons for the New Workplace

Richard A. Moran

The Updated Version

of the National Best Seller—

Never Confuse a Memo with Reality

 Heliotrope Books
New York City

It is possible to have an experience without sharing it.
        —Richard A. Moran

What used to be memories is now evidence.
        —The Eagles

I don't understand why any famous person would ever be on Twitter. The worst thing you can do is make yourself **more** *available.*
        —George Clooney

Heliotrope Books LLC
heliotropebooks@gmail.com

Cover Design by Judy Tipton-Katzman

Designed and Typeset by Naomi Rosenblatt with AJ&J Design

To the Family and All Those
Who Slug It Out Each and Every Day

Other Books by Richard A. Moran

Never Confuse a Memo with Reality
Beware Those Who Ask for Feedback
Cancel the Meetings, Keep the Doughnuts
Fear No Yellow Stickies
Nuts, Bolts and Jolts
Sins & CEOs

CONTENTS

Foreword   13

Introduction   16

Chapter One: Boiling Down Unwritten Work Rules
Showing Up Is Not a Skill   19

Chapter Two: My Cell Phone Is in the Toilet
Twitter, Social Media, Smart Phones,
and Other Addictions   35

Chapter Three: When Is Work Done?
Emails, Conference Calls, and Other Interruptions   48

Chapter Four: Buzzword Bingo and Bosses
Age, Gender, Sex, and Other Complications   61

Chapter Five: Manners and Meetings
Wasting Time Can Be Habit Forming   71

Chapter Six: Avoid the Seat Pocket in Front of You
Initiation Rites for the Business Traveller   89

Chapter Seven: Day by Day
Eating in Your Car and Other Tricks   99

Chapter Eight: Career Planning Is an Oxymoron
Running Through the Bushes and Brambles   109

Chapter Nine: Whatever Happened To?
Pagers and Other Collector's Items   127

Acknowledgements   131

About the Author   132

FOREWORD

I first met Rich Moran at a Starbucks in New York City on a cold winter day. Bundled as we were against my city's harsh winds, we each hailed a kindred spirit. It was clear that we shared more than the desire for grande latte: As big-time LinkedIn "Influencers," we've each risked evangelizing a business credo that upsets the common wisdom.

For example, we were taught to compete and "screw the rivals," but Rich and I believe in team playing and helping others to attain success. We were taught to ignore "the little guy" as we gun for bottom-line grandeur, but we value our customers and staff members and take time to hear them out. And we were taught to filch the glory of others, especially of talented underlings, but we give credit where it's due and return favors.

These are not merely our ideals, spouted naively in books and contradicted behind closed doors. Rich Moran and I are both CEOs who have put our standards to the test and made them work for our companies. We speak from the trenches, not the bully pulpit.

Along those lines, Rich and I are both passionate storytellers. Our lineages, renowned for their respective traditions of the parable and the yarn, have disposed each of us to appreciate the anecdote, and get a good one in wherever we can. Again and again, I delight in the "you-can't-make-this-stuff-up" aspect of Rich's cautionary corporate tales, or his reports of ironic success.

However, this new book is not composed of stories. Here you will find another Moran specialty: aphorisms, tips, and observations. They are based on the 355 aphorisms from *Never Confuse A Memo with Reality*, Rich's blockbuster book that was published in 1993 and continues to sell. Bringing it into the twenty-first century, Rich has revisited his adages with the aim of preserving some, while adding, amending, and deleting others.

These insights reflect the crazy essence of our workplace today and offer crisp, direct, witty, and always well-taken advice. Rich's words ring so true because they come from a veteran. As a CEO, venture capitalist, consultant for the likes of Apple, HP, News Corp, AT&T, and others, Rich has seen it all—or heard the buzz when he hasn't seen it.

His flow of adages will feel familiar to those who tweet. While Rich was neither a founder nor a creator of Twitter, his "bullet-pointed books" of the 1990s helped set the tone for this new form of communication. Succinct without being flippant long before the tweets began, Rich retains his belief in simplicity—not in the sense of simplification and "dumbing down," but in keeping to basic principles, like straight speaking and transparency. When I say that Rich Moran is likeable, you know that my endorsement doesn't get better.

In a world that assails us with fact and folly in real and in virtual time, simple phrases are often most memorable. Rich tells me that his publisher was struck by an assertion in his last book that "Getting to 80-percent right may be as good as it gets."

Now she often asks her staff: "Have we reached 'Rich Moran's 80 percent'?" And if so, it's a wrap and she knows not to break any backs in the illusory, often smothering pursuit of perfection.

I encourage readers to run with the sayings that resonate for you. Let them change your life, best your practices, and boost your corporate culture. Let them keep you out of trouble as you stay *in* the world, but not necessarily *of* it. Sit back, relax, and enjoy the tips, lessons, and musings to follow. But don't get so complacent that you miss the bearing of these deceptively simple phrases. May you enjoy success as you navigate daily through the tweets, feats, and deletes of our times.

—Dave Kerpen, 2014

Dave Kerpen is the CEO of Likeable Media and *New York Times* best-selling author of four books: *Likeable Social Media, Likeable Business, Likeable Leadership,* and *The Art of People.*

INTRODUCTION

Never Confuse a Memo with Reality was my first book and was written in a different world, in a different century, way back in the late '90s. It was a time before Twitter, Facebook, and a world of other venues and distractions. It was a time when I went on about the protocols for pagers and voice mail. It was a different time. No one writes memos, voicemail is now a necessary annoyance, and pagers are for physicians and drug dealers.

Never Confuse a Memo with Reality was also full of classic and simple advice. It became a best seller because as some told me, "It captured the unwritten codes of business." And it did. The book cut through the platitudes of how to be successful and told the truth about life in the workplace. It was easy to read and was useful when it came to correcting the behavior of bosses and coworkers. And that's why, even though it is out of date, it continues to be read by many.

So now it is time to update *Never Confuse a Memo with Reality.* I don't want it to become a collector's item. Memos are not a part of the new business parlance. (I considered changing the title to *Never Confuse a Tweet with Reality* or *Never Confuse Facebook with Reality* but there were too many legal challenges.)

The new version addresses the new workplace, which is now more confusing than ever. Work rules continue to change, but many classics are captured here. And many new issues will be explored here that were never a part of work before. Instead of waxing poetic about "car phones," it is time to worry about smart phones and other devices. Instead of worrying about voice mail messages piling up, we need to manage our text messages. Although the time elapsed between my original book and this update is not long, the list of what's new and what went away is a long one. To show how much the world has changed, I capture some of the classics here in the fun last section of this book, "Whatever Happened To?"

In many ways, the measures of success, both personal and organizational, never change. What changes is the route to get to that success and the environment in which the success is achieved. No matter how many new gadgets we have, embracing our career choice and enjoying work remain important.

A big frustration in today's workplace is the difficulty of measuring progress. The result of our work is often murky and can leave us feeling unsettled. It is a rare day when a decision is made. It is a rare sales meeting when something is sold. It is a rare event when you leave the office and proclaim, "Hot damn, that was a good day!" A day at work is more likely to be one full of returning emails with an occasional foray into Facebook. Then you get to the parking lot and proclaim, "WTF!, What did I do today?"

Stop! Work can be better. We need to acknowledge small achievements and convert nebulous defeats into minor victories. We need to make the choice to stake out the higher ground at work. We need to stop doing stupid things. We need to recognize that others notice how we behave.

Sometimes I wonder, *Is it me, or have people forgotten how to act? Or do they think no one is paying attention?* Technologies and the push-pull of home and career demands have made life complex and stressful, but that's not an excuse to grow into a rude bore.

If your courtesy and common sense quotient have atrophied, so probably have your career success and satisfaction. Whether the example is rude cell phone usage, two hundred-page PowerPoint presentations that no one will ever read, or heavy nasal breathing on conference calls, good judgment and proper behavior seem to be going in the wrong direction. This book is not a rant about cell phone usage or Facebook. It is, rather, a suggestion to take a deep breath (maybe on an airplane or in the shower, or at some other time of reflection) allow yourself time to consider the new and unwritten work rules—and retool your methods in some simple ways that can make your career and your life better.

ONE

BOILING DOWN UNWRITTEN WORK RULES

Showing Up Is Not a Skill

The workplace is changing so fast no one is sure what rules apply. Some think there are no rules anymore. Wrong. Being happy and successful means understanding rules. Those who pay attention to them tend to be appreciated and to move forward in their careers. To not know the rules or to avoid them creates career problems, even if you don't know it. And usually, if you are not paying attention to the rules, others don't tell you. Either because no one wants confrontation or others are perfectly willing to let you screw up.

Although there are some chestnuts that will always apply in the workplace, the rules will continue to change as long as technology and attitudes morph to make the workplace more effective.

1 Everyday at work is made up of ambiguous victories and nebulous defeats. Claim them all as ambiguous victories. Better to believe something has been accomplished, no matter how unclear, than to feel like you've wasted your time.

2 When everyone in the company walks around using the calculator function on the phone, it means people believe an IPO is about to be announced, or the stock price is going way up or way down. Or on the downside, an early retirement plan is in the works.

3 Driving to work and eating is the easiest way to gain weight. Donuts, pizza, and hamburgers are the meals of choice. Any food with the word "fast" around it is the fastest way to gain weight.

4 Sitting is the new smoking. Get up and get the blood flowing. Sitting and eating fast food at your desk is like smoking unfiltered Camel cigarettes.

5 Learn how to work at home without feeling like it is a day off. No one else thinks it is.

6 If you work from home a lot, never talk about daytime TV programs. Use the company VPN (virtual private network) when working from home. It is the way attendance is taken.

7 Only play music on your headphones that will make you more productive, not less.

8 Wearing headphones doesn't mean others have lost their hearing. Don't yell.

9 Get to know your coworkers, even in a workspace where wearing headphones is the norm. Take the headphones off so you can listen.

10 It is rare to take too many risks. Take more. If all of your ideas are working, you are not taking enough risks. Take on a new project, even if you are "in over your head."

11 The universal language in business is not English or Chinese. The universal language is PowerPoint. We now speak in the language of bullets and build slides. You must learn how to speak in PowerPoint, and you must learn how to pace yourself in a presentation.

12 Never say, "I know you can't read this but…" Show spreadsheets in a PowerPoint slide at your own peril.

13 Dogs at work are welcome when there are less than five employees. Dogs-at-work is not a model that scales well. In an office loaded with dogs, ask, "Which part of dogs at work do I like?" The poop? The dogs humping each other? The distractions? Or the dogs stealing the bagels intended for the staff meeting?"

14 Expect that anything you leave in a virtual office is fair game to pick through or get stolen. Don't decorate a virtual office. It is weird and there is no guarantee you will have the same space tomorrow.

15 If you come across a "personal" drawer in a virtual office (of the once full-time inhabitant), leave it alone.

16 Coffee and doughnuts are not a meal. Or should not be a meal.

17 "Gotta a minute?" is a signal that an interruption is coming.

18 "Gimme a minute" is a signal that you can wait.

19 Easy projects or easy sales are rare. If staff thinks that anything out there is easy to achieve, the result is like watching kindergarten soccer: everyone clusters around the ball.

20 Being known for having broad bandwidth is a compliment. It has nothing to do with your gender or height.

21 "One Size Fits All" is never true, with hats or with employee programs.

22 Acronyms are useful, but don't make up any. There are enough of them.

23 Big ideas may come out of the big offices, but most employees know that it is the small incremental ideas that make a big difference.

24 Finding quick hits or low-hanging fruit never is as easy as it seems. Ask any professional baseball player or fruit picker. Quick hits come from years of experience. Fruit pickers will pick the fruit at the top of the tree where it is riper.

25 Using spell-check is as important as wearing sunscreen. Reading the document after it has been through spell-check is as important as reapplying sunscreen.

26 Learn from our friends in Washington. Process doesn't matter as much as results. Posturing doesn't matter as much as results. Always try to answer the question, "What problem are we trying to fix?"

27 Employee turnover can have its virtues.

28 Any reorganization will mean some people will lose their jobs. Volunteer for the task force that will make recommendations about the reorganization.

29 Never go to more than two meetings a day or you will get nothing done.

30 Plan the day while you are in the shower. Don't take your electronic device into the shower with you.

31 Go to the company picnic. Don't stay long. Never sit in the dunk tank at the company picnic. Don't get drunk at the company picnic. Never dress up like a clown at Halloween.

32 The most successful people in business are often the most interesting.

33 Suspenders, bow ties, short skirts, cowboy boots, and big jewelry will always attract attention. Don't wear them if you don't want attention.

34 If you're dating someone in the office, don't expect anyone to talk to you about it. Do expect them to talk to each other about it.

35 There are very few places where you can get away with wearing a Hawaiian shirt. Hawaii is about it.

36 All that everyone always wants to know is the answer to three questions:
- What's my job?
- How am I doing?
- Does my contribution matter?

37 Never miss deadlines. Ever.

38 Ideas that didn't work are not a reason for an apology. Mistakes may require the apology.

39 Breakfast meetings are often very effective because there are fewer distractions. There is not much else to do, and people don't feel guilty for what they should have been doing. The price is getting up early.

40 Receptionists can always help you. If they don't like you, they can hurt you.

41 Make sure you have talent before you volunteer to perform at the company talent show.

42 Friday is becoming the new Saturday. Saturday is becoming the new Tuesday (just another work day).

43 Probationary periods don't exist. We are all on probation every day.

44 A whistle and a clipboard will often put you in charge.

45 Herewith the "List of Basics to Learn" (or what you need to know even though no one will ever tell you):

- Learn to read financial statements.
- Learn to write a proper email proposal, thank you, and summary.
- Learn to remember people's names. If your memory is poor, develop a system.
- Learn how to be comfortable around very senior managers, or learn to fake it.
- Learn how to build a spreadsheet and how to make a killer PowerPoint presentation.
- Learn how to run a meeting well and learn how to prepare an agenda.
- Learn to say, "I don't know." Especially if you don't know.
- Learn to use metaphors to convey your point.
- Learn how to build on ideas, and implement rather than find fault.

46 Nothing says more about what you think is important than your calendar.

47 Teamwork is the new currency of the workplace. Not being selected for a team is an unhappy indicator.

48 The fastest way to create organizational change is to change people.

49 Treating people like numbers will prevent the company from meeting its numbers.

50 If the response to your idea generates descriptors like "friction" or "high degree of difficulty," simplify it.

51 Develop a point of view about success—your own and your organization's.

52 Don't be afraid to ask the BIG (probably stupid) question; other people are probably wondering about it too.

53 The person who spends all of his or her time at work is not hardworking; he or she is boring.

54 Tweaking organizations will create a lot of tweaks but no real change.

55 Twerking employees will create a lot of news and some employee turnover.

56 Be known as someone who builds bridges, not fences or bombs.

57 Go to the company holiday party.

58 Don't get drunk at the company holiday party.

59 If you tell a racist joke, be prepared to be fired.

60 If you tell a racist joke, you should be fired.

TWO

MY CELL PHONE
IS IN THE TOILET

Twitter, Social Media, Smart Phones, and Other Addictions

Without being weird, look around in the bathroom. Although my experience is limited to the men's room, many of the guys in there are texting, reading email, or talking on their cell phone. The bathroom is just one place where the smart phone has entered our lives. It is here to stay, and the impact of the smart phone is immeasurable. It has affected work, relationships, productivity, and basically, everything we do. Some say the impact is for the worse, others think it is a miracle. In either case, knowing how and when to use a smart phone and other devices and gadgets will affect a career. The rules are constantly changing and still being written, so watch closely as more gadgets like Google glasses and wearable technology enter the workplace. There is no escape, there is no alternative; technology is changing the workplace and we are addicted.

61 Use your cell phone in the bathroom only if you have to call 911. There are exceptions.

62 All cell phones eventually end up in the toilet. Buying the waterproof case will save you trouble down the road.

63 Blocked access to websites at work will have people going to the bathroom more frequently to check websites on their smart phone. The blocked access makes productivity go down and more cell phones ending up in the toilet.

64 Cell phone use in the bathroom is already too rampant to stop. Nonetheless, some rules apply there too:
- Never use the "speaker" function while in a stall.
- Hit the mute button when the flusher takes action.

65 Ring tones can say more about you than you think. Be alert to what the rap song phrase may say when the phone rings in a meeting.

66 Never ever be the one who has the cell phone ring in church or in the movies. Turn it off.

67 If you have nothing to say, say nothing on social media. You will command much more attention when you do have something to say. Since EVERYONE has something to say all the time on all the platforms, restraint can be a virtue.

68 Everyone on LinkedIn is looking for a job. It is like being on American Idol, waiting to be discovered.

69 Look yourself up on the web to see if those college arrest photos are still there.

70 Put things in your calendar, even if you're absolutely positively sure you will remember them.

71 Restaurant cell phone etiquette is variable but certain rules do apply:
- Not a good idea on a date.
- Never a good idea if you want to enjoy the meal.

72 Keep track of how much time you waste between texting on your cell and checking in on social media, and think of how that time could be spent better. Writing a book? Solving world hunger? Redesigning the wait system at the DMV?

73 When you talk on cell phones in public, expect that everyone will be able to hear you; they will either be annoyed or listen in.

74 Don't give out your cell phone number unless you want people to call you on it. If colleagues do call and it is not a good time, tell them so.

75 Everyone on Facebook is either sailing, skiing, at the pool, or in a photo with George Clooney. It's not reality so don't let it get to you.

76 Be known as the one who writes the articles, not the snarky comments.

77 It's easier to check Facebook than to work. It's a trap, and an addictive one at that.

78 As far as my Facebook friends know, my life is perfect. It's not.

79 Facebook time does not equal face time.

80 Expect that your LinkedIn and Facebook profiles will be viewed by the following people, so make them accurate:

- Old girlfriends/boyfriends/ex-spouses
- Past employers
- The guy you competed with in your first job out of grad school
- Competitors
- Colleagues
- Your boss
- Old bosses
- Recruiters
- College Fund Raisers

81 Looking at Facebook can feel like you are looking at everyone else's highlight reel while you are laboring in the outtakes.

82 It is a small world and getting smaller, and there are an even smaller number of people who count.

83 There are no more "blind dates." Your date will know everything about you via Facebook/Twitter/LinkedIn before you even meet. Same with your future employers.

84 Instead of airing complaints on Facebook, try reaching out to a friend via phone or text.

85 Know how to use the map apps on all of your devices. We all need to know where we are going, where other people are, or how to just plan an escape. Never have more than one map app talking to you at the same time.

86 Always call ahead or send a text to tell people you will be late. It's one of the many reasons why communications devices were invented.

87 On certain occasions there is no substitution for a call. A tweet, a text, or a post won't convey the true sentiment.

88 Unless you are talking, of course, when you're on a conference call on a cell phone, always hit the mute button. It will kill the background noise and the heavy breathing. Know how to turn the mute button on and off quickly and in the dark.

89 Post things. Not all things. Not every minute or every hour. Your lunch is never interesting to others.

90 If you're feeling sorry for yourself, use your device to find people who are in situations way worse than yours. They won't be hard to find. Don't look at others' vacation pictures or happy love lives.

91 Borrowing someone's cell phone is ok to find lost friends, call for pizza deliveries, or call 911. Otherwise is it like borrowing someone's toothbrush.

92 Memorize the phone keypad so that you can spell names and dial numbers without looking at it.

93 Hashtag overuse on Twitter is akin to spamming your followers.

94 Naming a child based on URL availability may not result in a name that the child will want. But it does guarantee a unique domain name.

95 Think of your followers and those who you're follow-ing on Twitter as a garden, and regularly cut the dead-heads.

96 Look up from the smart phone when crossing streets and at kids' soccer games. The text can wait.

97 Don't assume social media networks will take the place of the network of personal friends and others who can help you.

98 Social media will guarantee you receive email from someone you don't want to hear from. Some from people you know, many from those you hope you never know.

99 Social media allows us to create daily reunions—without the heavy drinking.

100 If your meal partner takes out a cell phone and puts it on the table, take yours out too. It's like putting the six-shooter on the table.

101 If you don't want to, or can't talk, don't answer the phone.

102 Facebook has replaced daytime television as a way to kill the day.

103 Posting anything on any social media site will have you checking that site every two minutes for the next day to see who likes it or shares it.

104 The best feeling in the world is to have all devices fully charged and raring to go.

105 Broadcasting a "selfie" can sometimes be akin to wearing the T-shirt that says, "Been there, done that, have this T-shirt to prove it."

THREE

WHEN IS
WORK DONE?

Emails, Conference Calls, and Other Interruptions

It is hard to keep up. Every day is busy, every day is booked solid. We keep track of our time on fancy gadgets and devices. But do we spend our time on the most important activities during the day? The answer is probably a resounding no. Somehow the job does get done but it may require cheating. That can include doing real work while you're on conference calls. Or working on a project while you're in a meeting on a different subject. Or not ever taking a lunch so you can do what you are supposed to. Or—least desirable—doing your job at night because you can't get anything done during the day. We all work out our own little tricks. A few generic tricks may help you cope with the distractions and focus on the priorities.

106 Read your email soon after you receive it and respond quickly. The old rule of twenty-four hours to respond is way out. Depending on the organization, response time is measured by others—overtly or not. Some say three hours is the new mean, but in some organizations five minutes is too long.

107 "Message erased" is as good as "checked that one off."

108 "Message marked private" can make the heart skip a beat.

109 The production of a brochure never solves a business problem or generates sales. An online presence and social media activities are what now matter.

110 Email is one of the best efficiency tools ever created. It is not a source of guilt. Don't skip emails that make you feel guilty or like you have done something wrong—and especially don't store them. The problem won't go away. Read the message, see what needs to be done, respond to the message, and take care of the problem.

111 When someone sends you an announcement about his or her new job or promotion, send a note of congratulations. LinkedIn messages can work.

112 Be known as someone who can use an app or go into system preferences and change things.

113 Email is a communications tool, not a management technique.

114 The "permanent record" used to be a vague threat about a file in the school principal's office. Now the permanent record is real and is everywhere on the Internet. Always think twice before hitting the send button.

115 If the number of email messages is overwhelming, take them in batches of five or ten. Avoid skipping the mean or onerous ones. The one with the most emails is not the winner.

116 The number of emails you receive is directly proportional to the number of emails you send. The more you send, the more you get.

117 Expect most people to respond to email long before voice mail. Remember that a voice mail message marked "private" cannot be forwarded, but it can still be transcribed..

118 Expect that every message you send or receive is being monitored.

119 Being efficient could mean that you end your day with zero unopened emails or unanswered voice mails. Being effective means you measured your day in what you accomplished, not in emails, texts, and returned voice mails.

120 Don't stop doing real work every time your computer beeps with new email.

121 Assume that any attachment to an email message will be neither launched, detached, nor read.

122 Pay attention to the "RE:" line in email and make it specific to the message. Sometimes a little creativity there won't hurt; just don't make your email appear like spam.

123 Sending lewd material out via email will get you fired. And no, not just pornography, but bad stuff. You know it when you see it.

124 Adding more systems to a bad system makes a bigger bad system.

125 In some emails, the only thing that matters are the "CCs."

126 Send/Delete/Repeat is a rhythm to get into when facing 100+ email messages.

127 "Reply All" can be the most dangerous option on the screen.

128 Never confuse an email with reality...most emails from the top don't change the work you do.

129 If you're going to project onto a large screen, make sure one of your desktop icons is not labeled "porn."

130 "I erased it" are three of the sorriest words in the English language. Other sorry words include "I am not a racist but..." and "It hurts me to say this but..."

131 Never get dressed up for a conference call.

132 Learn how to use Skype so you don't appear to be at the wrong end of a telescope.

133 When giving a presentation, don't stand in the dark, or people will think you are *in* the dark. Speak from an area where people will see you.

134 The talk-show-host approach of mingling and working with the audience doesn't always work.

135 Not everything requires a PowerPoint presentation. A presentation can imply limited options and inhibit useful discussions.

136 Fix your computer setup so that you don't have to crawl around under your desk to plug it in. Doubly important if you have to get dressed up for work.

137 Going global means middle-of-the night-conference calls.

138 Conference calls are the premium time for multi-tasking. It may be the only time when you can get work done.

139 Write down computer passwords somewhere. Probably not on your computer.

140 Tech Support taking away your computer for upgrades with promises that you will never notice the changes is like the dentist saying there will be some discomfort.

141 Be the first to use technologies. Introduce new technologies to the workplace and informally train people on them. Be the one who "really" understands social media.

142 Even in a virtual world, never underestimate how important it is that people talk to each other. Not because they have to but because they want and need to.

143 Message boards are a questionable source of information and gossip about any organization, especially the stock price. Recognize that it is the bucket for every bitch and gripe and not a repository for the positive.

144 Headphones at work may help you concentrate and may be relaxing. Headphones can also be a way to hide and are not good for making friends.

145 Weekend conference calls will guarantee dogs barking and children crying in the background. And resentful participants.

146 If there is heavy breathing on a conference call, the host should gently ask that someone apply nasal strips, wake up, turn off the porno movie, or move the receiver away from their face.

147 Conference calls are always better than an airplane seat.

148 There should be one slide for every five minutes of talk, not five slides for every one minute of talk. What you don't present will never been seen. Be thankful if what you do present is seen.

149 It's a cliché to say, "The Internet is changing how we work ..." or "In our rapidly changing (economy, world ...)." Everyone knows it. Start with something we don't know.

150 The Executive Summary is often the only thing that is read in any document. Make sure it tells a good story.

151 The most dreaded phrases in any presentation are, "These numbers don't look right" or "Can we do a process check?"

FOUR

BUZZWORD BINGO AND BOSSES

Age, Gender, Sex, and Other Complications

Just as the workplace is going through mind-numbing changes, so is the world of leadership and management. The techniques that worked ten years ago no longer apply. Managers today need to be both smart **and** quick. Leaders today need to be both self-aware and inspirational. Every social media site is jam-packed with advice about how to be better if you are the boss. Big initiatives that require implementation like Six Sigma, Total Quality Management, Employee Participation, and big systems (or Big Systems) have all been done. Now what?

Great managers and effective leaders are hard to come by, but that is nothing new. What is new is the relationships between managers and others. Autocrats are dying. Bullies are demonized and fired. New roles and rules are emerging. Results always matter but the means to get those results is a real "work in process."

152 Buzzwords are part of business language. They may be annoying but often serve as shorthand and currency. Besides the old standards like Outside the Box, Low-hanging Fruit, and Connecting the Dots, know about Advertainment, Social learning, Return on Involvement, Inventreprenuers, Twinternship, and Triti-tasking. The list will never end.

153 Buzzwords are like top forty songs. At first, they bring a smile or capture a thought, but pretty soon you're sick of them.

154 Early adopters and early adapters are not the same. Adopters are the risk takers. Adapters are the incrementalists.

155 The most effective suggestion system is the one where the CEO actually reads the email from employees.

156 Never underestimate how fast a strategy will outlive its usefulness.

157 Opening phrases of letters that invariably mean something bad is about to happen to you include:
- Due to increased …
- Due to decreased …
- Reported attempts …
- Based on our records …
- Unfortunately …

158 While on LOA, including maternity, talk to your boss occasionally while you're gone so he or she is not surprised when you come back.

159 If your boss says, "your job is to make me look good," it probably is.

160 Keep any and all thank-you emails from customers and present them at review time.

161 Poor performers require ten times more time than solid performers to get the job done.

162 Poor performers who are in denial about their performance require fifty times more time to get the job done.

163 Work on problems, not symptoms. Morale itself is never a problem; something is happening that causes low morale, which creates problems.

164 "Actions follow intent" is the only phrase that needs completion to have a strategy. If you intend to lose weight you act like you are on a diet.

165 If your boss is giving your name out to search people, it's probably time to exercise some job-hunting initiative of your own.

166 If you tell your new boss to take a number and get in line because you have so many bosses, the organization is overly matrixed.

167 Never complicate—especially processes and procedures.

168 Worry more about implementation than strategy—it's harder to do.

169 Not utilizing the skills of employees is the worst sin of management.

170 Lack of credibility will hurt more than lack of quality.

171 Never let your guard down around the bosses—especially when traveling or socializing. Assume anything juicy posted online will be seen.

172 Understand how pay and bonuses are administered and how decisions are made regarding pay. That knowledge could save some heartache at raise time.

173 The one thing that management always reads is the All Employee Surveys. Especially the comments about leadership.

174 No one likes performance reviews but always be prepared when the event comes around. Do your own review in advance and give it to your boss.

175 The best mission statement ever written is that of Federal Express: To deliver the package the very next morning, regardless.

176 If your performance review is the same year after year, you either have a very boring job or no one is really doing your review.

177 Yellow stickies left on computer screens at night with cryptic messages are not a substitute for management or communications.

178 In a management shake-up, if no one loses his or her job, it is not a shakeup. If low paid employees are the only ones to lose their jobs, nothing was shaken.

179 Never babysit the children of your boss.

180 Get to work thirty minutes before your boss.

181 There are no such things as communications, turnover, or morale problems. They are symptoms of bigger problems. Fix the problem, not the symptom.

182 Incremental change should take weeks or months, not years.

183 Finding fault in others is way less interesting than building on the ideas of others.

184 All budgeting processes are disliked. Understand the process and what it means to your group. Never miss a budget deadline.

185 Don't confuse the organizational chart with who does what. Real activity often takes place in the white space between the organizational chart lines.

186 The creation of any organization is a series of compromises.

187 Rejoice in the successful completion of projects and major activities. Remember how it felt to put the calculus text away for the last time knowing you'd never have to open it again.

FIVE

MANNERS AND MEETINGS

Wasting Time Can Be Habit Forming

If you stacked all the books and guides on how to run a meeting they would reach to the moon. Sometimes I doubt anyone has read any of them. Meetings continue to be the source of frustration and wasted time in all organizations. (Although there is a population that believes meeting time is the only time when things get done, if they don't pay attention to the meeting agenda and work on emails.)

A few simple guidelines about managing meetings are outlined in this chapter. But meetings are not the only frustration we face at work. The list is long depending on the workplace: it could be smelly coworkers, broken cappuccino machines, or bully bosses. Trust me, no workplaces are frustration-free.

188 Putting your company's name on a vanity license plate is risky. At some point you might be driving a vehicle with a plate broadcasting the company that fired you.

189 Building an entire wardrobe on branded apparel is a good way to broadcast your company and your role. Be proud of your company and wear the clothes like a badge. Just be ready to change wardrobes.

190 If you're becoming good friends with the night custodian and you have a day job, you are working too hard.

191 Eliminate annoying habits like cracking your knuckles, smacking your lips, belching and catching it in your mouth, licking your fingers, and talking to yourself. All your neighbors in close proximity will appreciate it.

192 When someone says, "Don't worry—you're young, marketable, and willing to relocate," it's time to worry.

193 A sigh can often be the key indicator as to whether work will get done, and how effectively.

194 Don't treat people like they are dead if they get laid off or fired.

195 If trust is a "corporate value" that requires verification, there's a lot of work to do before true trust happens.

196 The size of your office is not as important as the size of your paycheck. Not having an office can be fine if there is a good reward.

197 The best thing about making lists is crossing things off. Make lists every day. Cross things off every hour.

198 If you accomplish something significant that's not on your list, write it down so you can cross it off.

199 Find a "walk-up" song and listen to it daily. Listen to Copeland's "Fanfare for the Common Man" every Monday morning. AC/DC's "Back in Black" may be the Friday afternoon "walk-up" song.

200 When waiting in the lobby for a meeting, don't sit down. Sitting can take your "edge" away and you will be at a physical disadvantage when it is time to greet.

201 If you write an email to someone above you in the chain of command, risks abound, but so do awards.

202 The word "whatever" is properly used in the phrase, "Whatever it takes," never as in "Whatever!" Saying "whatever" means you don't care; or you don't believe the decision is already made; or you don't know any other words; or the worst—you are resigned to cynicism. None of these definitions is attractive. All choices matter; it is never "Whatever."

203 Even with mature products and processes, look for the simple ideas that make for dramatic improvements, like the little green thingy that slides into the lid of cups at Starbucks.

204 Never complain about clients or customers unless you are 100 percent sure it will never get back to clients or customers.

205 You can never be 100 percent sure that complaints will not get back to clients or customers.

206 Bumper stickers not to post in your cubicle:
- Jesus is coming, everyone look busy.
- Reality is a crutch for people who can't handle drugs.
- My kid had sex with your honor student.
- If you're not outraged, you're not paying attention.

207 Squatter's rights don't count when it comes to reserved conference rooms.

208 Don't hang your diplomas in your office unless you are an M.D.

209 Use no more than two of the following words in the same sentence: *value, delivery, quality, strategic, global,* or *paradigm.*

210 There are multifunction and single function breaks at meetings. Let people know if it's just the bathroom, just the phones, just the coffee, or all three. All breaks at meetings last longer than they are supposed to.

211 Never assume everyone has hung up from a conference call before you start a private conversation with those who admit to still being on the line.

212 Responding to Requests for Proposals is not as bad as everyone tells you, but worse than you think.

213 "Agree in concept" is usually a long way from "I agree."

214 A casual, "We can do that," often means the scope has changed and it will show up on the next bill.

215 Behavior that you wouldn't want your mom, brother, or sister subjected to is probably harassment. No need for big legal manuals or policies; use the family test as your guide.

216 Remove the ink stamp on the back of your hand that you got at the bar last night before you show up for work.

217 Reputations last a long time, maybe forever. Get a reputation for doing what is always right.

218 "W2 envy" will drive you crazy and is not worthy of the brain space. And like penis envy, there's not much you can do about it.

219 Jabbing the elevator button incessantly will not make the elevator appear faster. Go to the bathroom before you get on the elevator.

220 Secrets in any organization are never kept. No matter how many "I will not tell . . ." documents are signed and bibles sworn upon, there are no secrets.

221 If you are in an employee focus group, make sure you trust everyone before you speak your mind. Then be careful what you say.

222 Even in a virtual office, show up. Just know what showing up means. It could mean conference calls, logging into email, discharging voice mail, or chitchatting with your assistant.

223 All meeting agendas are tentative.

224 No matter how long the meeting, the good stuff will all happen at the end.

225 Never be late for meetings. If you are late, just apologize and move on.

226 Time sheets are the one absolute in a billable environment. If they are required, get them in on time.

227 Some meetings are like listening to a long line of radio commercials only to hear the song you hate.

228 Politics can convert a one-hour meeting into an eight-hour meeting with no result.

229 Leading a meeting and facilitating a meeting are not the same.

230 If a colleague mentions a "partner" at home, don't ask if it's a man or a woman.

231 Never wordsmith in a meeting. You have better things to do.

232 Special approvals make for special delays.

233 When you hear anything close to, "We're not going to get any smarter about this," just make the best decision you can.

234 If you have to ask if there is a conflict of interest, there probably is.

235 No one is measured by the number of meetings he or she attended during a year.

236 Ask for input only if you really want it and plan to do something with it.

237 Treat your time as if someone is paying for it. Someone is.

238 Read your job description occasionally but never be restricted by it. Do what needs to be done.

239 Never start a meeting or a retreat with a blank sheet of paper. Know what the outcome options are and work to decide on one.

240 Ask for questions only if you want them.

241 Those who do the work should have a say in how it is to be organized.

242 Without the "right" people in the meeting, there will be more than one meeting.

243 The "cycle of performance" for careers is shortening. You are only as good as your last project.

244 If you're in a job where someone ever tells you to look busy, look for another job.

245 Strive to be known as a: Rainmaker, People Developer, or Decision Maker.

246 Never let anyone you work with see you naked.

247 Keep a toothbrush and toothpaste on hand and use them.

248 Reheating last night's dinner in the company microwave will always get the attention of others—maybe not in a good way. Watch out for burritos and Chinese food.

249 The fastest way to create organizational change is to change the people.

250 No standards + no measures + no penalties = no direction.

251 Right place/right time is rarely an accident or coincident.

252 Use New Year's Eve and Back to School time as a way of setting and resetting goals.

253 Don't be afraid to collect payment for outstanding bills. It may be the most onerous, but most important, part of your job.

254 Never in your life say, "It's not my job."

255 Always sit at the conference table. Never on the wall or in the "peanut gallery." That's like sitting at the kid's table.

256 Don't ask colleagues if they dye their hair. Don't tell them they are fat, bald, look pregnant, or look tired. Always compliment or say nothing at all.

SIX

AVOID THE SEAT POCKET IN FRONT OF YOU

Initiation Rites for the Business Traveller

It's no fun, everyone agrees. Business travel is not for the meek—they do not inherit the First-Class upgrade. This entire book could be about the perils of travel and the prescriptions for making the best of it. And that's all we can expect—making the best of a bad situation. So grin and bear it. Bear with the delays. Bear with the small seats and the guy in front of you who slams his seat back. Bear with no overhead space for your luggage. Bear with having gold elite turbo status and never getting upgraded. Bear with the de-icings. There are not a lot of options if you really need to be there.

257 Anytime you read *USA Today*, people around you will assume you spent last night in a hotel.

258 If the sound of the zipper on your luggage makes your children cry, you're traveling too much.

259 If the airline agent calls you to the counter, something either very good or very bad is about to happen.

260 Don't make airline delay stories as long as the delay.

261 You're on too many airplanes if you can't sleep without a seat belt on or, if while in bed, you try to put a seat belt around your blanket so the flight attendants can see it.

262 Never expect to find an available outlet in an airport that will allow you to recharge your devices; if you do it is a bonus.

263 Airport parking is stressful enough. Make sure you know height limits before you get in line to park your SUV with the big roof rack on the top.

264 Airplane Cart Management is when you time your visits to the bathroom so that you don't interfere with food or beverage carts.

265 Sometimes the most productive work is done when stuck in an airport near an electrical outlet.

266 Mending kits and shoe mitts from hotels never count as gifts. Regardless of the age of the recipient.

267 First-class flights mean never having to check an appropriate-sized carry-on.

268 Kill time on the "where you need to be" end, not the "where you're leaving from end."

269 Give up on trying to work on your computer and eat airplane food at the same time.

270 The most dreaded words for the very experienced business traveler, that group who has memorized the 800-number for all airline reservation services:
- Unfortunately
- Good news and bad news
  (the good news never counts)
- Shuttle bus
- Talking to maintenance
- Reservation was not guaranteed
- DO you have a confirmation number
- Trying a new menu
- That bag has to be checked
- The President is in town

271 Never tell someone on an airplane to keep his or her baby quiet.

272 Expect to get in a fistfight with anyone you tell to keep a baby quiet.

273 Rejoice if you don't have to take a shuttle bus to get to the rental car place.

274 Be realistic about how much work you can accomplish at night or on a day trip and only pack that much. Bags and briefcases are always over-packed based on productivity optimism.

275 Even if you travel more than they do, flight attendants don't want to hear your travel war stories.

276 Know where all the public restrooms are on the routes you usually travel to clients or work.

277 If you're going to watch the movie on an airplane, get the headphones.

278 Call home every night when you are on the road.

279 Be prepared to lose anything that you place in "the seat pocket in front of you."

280 Expect never to see anything you leave on an airplane again.

281 There are two ways to travel—first class or with children.

282 Always allow more time than you think to get to the airport. Especially in New York City.

283 Airplane crash jokes are not funny.

284 Never travel in first class if your boss or the customer you are traveling with are not. Even if you are being upgraded and they aren't.

285 Use airplane time to reflect and set personal goals. It may be the only quiet time you ever get.

286 Never complain about the de-icing process during a blizzard.

287 Always keep your passport and airline ticket in the same place or pocket.

288 At most, only half the time you spend on an airplane will be productive. Plan accordingly.

289 When going through security, always get behind the guy wearing loafers.

SEVEN

DAY BY DAY

Eating in Your Car and Other Tricks

Showing up and doing something productive for a wage—that's work. It is everything else that can make life at work miserable or a joy. Dealing with all the "else" is the trick and the secret to success. Lots of advice is available on how to deal with distractions, annoying coworkers, time management, and crazy bosses. Dealing with all work issues on a day-to-day basis can be stressful and sometimes you just have to strike a balance between focusing on what you are supposed to be doing and dealing with all else.

Making good small decisions is the difference between success and just being average in the workplace.

290 Benefits (the healthcare kind) are a big reason to get and keep a job now. Understanding healthcare now is like understanding college-level calculus.

291 Sometimes procrastination can get you out of doing what you don't want to. Don't always count on it.

292 Always know who your client or customer is—no matter what your job and no matter where the customer is located—online or right in front of you. If you have a paying client, you have a job.

293 Setting expectations with people is the most important part of business. That includes employees, customers, clients, suppliers, consultants, and anyone related to the success of the business. Really tell the truth.

294 When making organizational or personal change, it often doesn't matter where you start. Just start.

295 Quick and thorough implementation is a strategy. The winners know how to implement.

296 When putting those Value Statements together, it's not worth debating the relative importance of integrity, honesty, and trustworthiness. It doesn't matter; they are all important.

297 If business plans are not clearly communicated, it doesn't mean they don't exist.

298 The harder it is to create a deck for potential investors, the more likely it is that what the company is all about is not clear. Try understanding what the business really and truly does before the pitch begins.

299 Don't confuse spreadsheets with analysis, or documentation with diligence.

300 Sometimes it's easier and cheaper to try something and see what happens rather than waste time and money to study and analyze it forever.

301 Don't try to be close friends with subordinates. They don't expect to be friends with their boss, and it makes it harder to make people decisions.

302 Going in to the office when it's dark and leaving when it's dark should only apply for a few weeks in December. Don't measure yourself or anyone else by how much time is spent in the office.

303 Presentation skills and storytelling are keys to career growth, getting funded, and personal confidence. Develop a good style and always be the one who the team wants to give the presentation.

304 When working out of your home, get up and take a shower and get dressed as if you were about to go somewhere. You'll be productive faster.

305 An organization with a reputation that it eats their young and shoots their old is not one to work for unless you are forty years old and plan to stay that way forever.

306 If your job is like playing "Bop the Mole," remember that even though they all pop up, not all the moles are the same size.

307 Rules from the Work World that Apply to All Teenagers:
- Always let someone know where you are.
- Leaving a message or sending a text doesn't mean you have permission.
- Be home when you say you will. Period.
- Know what is absolutely non-negotiable. Like, "Give me the car keys."
- If you're in trouble, don't negotiate.

308 Never underestimate the power of a parking place and never take it for granted.

309 Never underestimate the wrath you can incur by taking more than one parking place.

310 Take the time from work to go to your child's plays, recitals, games, and special events even if the child is the youngest of ten.

311 Don't speak on cell phones on the sidelines of your child's games. Be the listener, and rejoice that the mobile device is the enabler that allows you to be there.

312 The "Out of Office" note is from the '90s. No one believes that you are not still checking messages.

313 When trying to schedule a meeting for more than two, no time is ever good for all. Forget trying to find the perfect time.

314 Food to never eat in you car on the way to a meeting:
- Burritos
- Whoppers
- Jelly Doughnuts

315 If your friends accuse you of having a "Century-At-a-Glance" calendar, you may be too anal about planning your time.

316 Even if it requires an engineer for help, fix your office chair so that it is comfortable. Don't sit in it all day. Get up and move around.

317 Rock bottom is always deeper and lower than you think.

318 Build on your strengths and improve them. Do the best you can with your weaknesses.

319 Never give a bad reference. If you have nothing good to say, don't say anything—that will be message enough.

320 Morale doesn't necessarily improve when the news for the organization is good.

321 Use commuting time well. Learn something or do something (that will not make you a dangerous driver).

322 Realistic planning is a good way to reduce stress and pressure.

323 Although you don't know it at the time, where you go to college can affect your career in many ways. All decisions have implications.

324 If you believe you have no future, you don't.

EIGHT

CAREER PLANNING IS AN OXYMORON

Running Through the Bushes and Brambles

Not everyone is a computer engineer who wants to live in Silicon Valley. Not everyone realized at the age of four that he or she wanted to grow up to be a brain surgeon. Some of us are lucky enough to stumble into something that we love and for which we get paid. But in general, both career planning and the actual job search are entirely hit-or-miss endeavors. To make matters worse, choosing careers and finding jobs can be totally confusing with so many choices and so many venues to explore. Technology makes it worse because it can give us the illusion that we are actually doing something.

The grand lesson in both choosing a career and finding a job is that it is all about you. Others can advise and help but it is you who must take control of your own career. In the end, it is you who chooses and makes decisions along the way. Enjoy the journey.

325 Some things have not changed since choosing up teams on the playground. If you are not getting chosen, develop the skill that will get you chosen. When you hear your name associated with phrases like "on the bench," "on the beach," or "underutilized," work on your skills, not being more available.

326 When assessments start taking place that label people "revenue generators" or "non-revenue generators," those labeled non-revenue should worry about their jobs.

327 While looking for a job, make sure that all your devices are working in case someone wants to reach you. Double check all sites for any recent posts on new jobs. Sometimes being first in line matters.

328 The word "gofer" should never be used when describing experience. There are much better ways to describe the skills involved in getting coffee.

329 Learn the difference between marketing, sales, public relations, and advertising. Then learn again about how each of those functions works online.

330 When you get the entrepreneurial urge, go visit someone who's started a business—it may cure you.

331 Do something fantastic early in any new job or assignment. It counts more in the early going.

332 Remember that job security does not exist. Maybe it never did.

333 Resume gimmicks rarely work. Most resumes are read by machines and responses are rare. It's the key words that count.

334 Gather a "personal board of directors," a group that will provide advice and counsel. It can be real or virtual. The question becomes, "What would (fill in the blank) do in this situation?

335 If you change jobs frequently in a short period of time by either getting fired or quitting, there might be more going on than just meeting the futurists' predications that we will all have eight careers in our lifetime.

336 Don't appear on any talk show when they're talking about "Bosses from Hell," unless you have just won the lottery.

337 In describing your job, if the typical response is "Nice work if you can get it" or "Live the dream," keep your job.

338 The process of negation is sometimes the best way to make a decision. Knowing what you don't want might get you what you want.

339 Make sure you get proper credit for previous work experience before you start any new job. Once you start, the negotiations are over.

340 Two things matter in an internship—try to get both:
- The brand of where you toiled.
- The experience you can describe later.

341 Going virtual and hoteling make it easier to quit because you don't have to worry about cleaning out your office.

342 Repeatedly saying "someday," "sometime," and "one of these days" is a sign it may be time for a career change.

343 There are no jobs, only career choices.

344 If all that is said is, "... to pursue other interests," everyone will ask what really happened.

345 Being labeled as a Subject Matter Expert (SME) is almost always the sign that you know more in that area, and no one else is going to bother to learn since they already have an expert. Become an SME only in something that you like to talk about.

346 All candidates for any job need to be sold, no matter how special you believe your organization to be.

347 Consider all jobs as immersion programs. Being a lifeguard could be an immersion program in oceanography and first aid. Being an executive assistant could be an immersion project in project management and dealing with buttheads.

348 If you father or mother runs the company, be the first one in and the last one out every day.

349 Don't choose a job based on it having the latest start date. Or the earliest one.

350 Bad bosses make for bad jobs. Good bosses make for better jobs.

351 In your performance review, if you hear the phrase, "Sets low standards and consistently fails to meet them," look for another job.

352 Career questions that include the word "still" puts a tentative at best or negative at worst value on the career question. As in "Are you still selling life insurance?" No one hears the question, "Are you still a brain surgeon?" Beware the word "still".

353 If people say you are working in the white space, they probably don't know what you do.

354 Be free and expansive with career advice for colleague's children. Someday your own children will be looking for good advice.

355 When you change jobs and everyone tells you that they are writing your new number in pencil, think again.

356 Surfing between job-hunting websites and porno websites will leave you confused. And without a job.

357 Employers really do hire from their websites. Learn how to use them even if you never hear back from anyone.

358 Falsifying your resume on the web is as bad as falsifying on paper—only faster. Either one can get you fired.

359 Bad first jobs are like bad first dates. They may last longer than you had hoped.

360 Making good decisions about your career direction is better than sitting around at home watching daytime television.

361 Continuing in a career that is "only OK" is like dating someone you know you will never marry.

362 A bad job where you are learning something and making money is better than being idle.

363 When you get fired give yourself two days to feel sorry for yourself. Focus on your next job, not your last one.

364 Spend job-hunting time with people who can hire you or refer you to people who can hire you. It's too easy to waste time.

365 The most devastating word for job seekers is "unfortunately."

366 The hiring process always takes longer than both seekers and employers want.

367 Landing a job is as much a function of timing as it is qualifications.

368 Never tell the person interviewing you that he or she reminds you of a golden retriever or other animals.

369 Being the last one to leave a company that is going downhill is good and bad. Good for loyalty, bad for timing.

370 "Salary is secondary to challenge, growth, and opportunity," is one of the great lies of the world.

371 When requested to attend a meeting at 4:30 on Friday, and to bring your badge and laptop, don't go.

372 The fastest way to give yourself a raise is to work fewer hours.

373 Never curse during an interview, even if the interviewer does.

374 "Individual contributor" is a label to avoid if you want to be promoted. It usually means people think you lack the ability to lead a project or team.

375 Remembering other's names could get you promoted. Sneaking glances at name tags will broadcast that you don't know names.

376 Being part of a growing company does not ensure career growth. But it helps.

377 Once you quit or retire, stay away from the old workplace. They don't miss you.

378 "Interim" is usually not a good spot to be in.

379 Wear nose rings only if you work for MTV, a messenger service, or for yourself.

380 When you hear words like "restructuring," "de-layering", and/or "rightsizing," think about getting your resume together.

381 Know what your pay grade is—what the salary range is, where you are in the range, and how to get to the next level.

382 Have lunch once a month with someone outside the company who someday might hire you.

383 Money now is worth more than money later.

384 If a job sounds too good to be true, it probably is.

385 A good raise is 5 percent. A great raise is 10 percent.

386 Career planning is an oxymoron; the most exciting opportunities tend to be unplanned.

387 Even if you are a great performer, if you quit your job and then change your mind and want to go back, don't expect to get rehired.

388 Inside a career are many choices. Always choose to do what you will remember ten years from now.

389 When choosing a major in college, if you don't enjoy the subject or the classes, you won't like the career.

390 Help others network for jobs. What goes around comes around.

391 If you are worried about your job, you probably should be.

392 If others tell you to worry about your job, you really should.

393 Always have an answer to the question, *What would I do if I lost my job tomorrow?*

NINE

WHATEVER HAPPENED TO...

Pagers and Other Collector's Items?

Take a look at any "success" book from any time in the past—recent or not so recent. You might learn about collar stays or waxing moustaches. Or you might learn about the proper care and oiling of Rolodex files or card catalogues. It wasn't all that long ago that we wore pagers that beeped like crazy, and walked to work wearing a Sony Walkman thinking we were cool. The workplace continues to change so quickly that someday readers will review this book and look back in wonder at how backward we were in efficiency and productivity. In fact, in reviewing an earlier edition of the book, I am struck by how fast things have changed.

The following are classics from the past bullets that will make you chuckle, together with a few side comments of my own.

- When working from home, check in with your boss every day. (*Today your boss doesn't want you to check in.*)

- When traveling with your boss, make sure you have good directions. If you get lost you will get blamed. (*GPS and Google Maps made that bullet an antique.*)

- Never play a Walkman so loud that the people around you can hear it. (*Everyone around you is probably wearing earphones so it doesn't matter.*)

- Phone messages should not be allowed to pile up. (*No one makes phone calls any more.*)

- If there is no slide on the overhead, turn the projector off. (*What's an overhead?*)

- Never leave the men's room with your tie slung over your shoulder. (*Most workplaces don't worry about ties. Lots of guys think wearing a tie is reserved for weddings and funerals. If that.*)

- Be known as someone who can set a VCR timer and will do so rather than watch 12:00 blink incessantly. (*Thank goodness VCRs were obsolete before anyone learned how to program them.*

- In these days of the Internet and tech breakthroughs, be joyous if you can connect to your office network from a remote location. (*Joy abounds today.*)

- Always turn your computer on when you're in the office—even if all it shows is toasters flying by. (*I liked those toasters. All computers are now always on.*)

- The size of your office is not as important as the size of your paycheck. (*What's an office?*)

- Carry telephone numbers with you. (*See below.*)

- Never go into a meeting without your calendar. (*The calendar, the contacts, and the research of the universe is now in one little place—your phone.*)

- Don't leave the newspaper on the bathroom floor. Don't take it there in the first place. (*What's a newspaper? But the message is still the same: don't spend all day in the bathroom.*)

ACKNOWLEDGMENTS

I owe a big debt of gratitude to all those in the work world who continue to do stupid things or break the most basic rules of business common sense. It is a long list too long to publish. It is a list also that continues to grow every week. Coming closer to home, I am grateful to Naomi Rosenblatt who is more than patient and supportive. The team at SNP Communications in San Francisco helped with the cool new stuff and how brought perspective to what would be of interest to the "young groovers." The Family always advises me to curb my language and provides perspective on titles. And to all those who send me suggestions and ideas, thanks.

ABOUT THE AUTHOR

Richard A. Moran is a nationally known authority on corporate leadership and workplace issues. He is a CEO, a venture capitalist, board member, and a consultant to major corporations. His CBS radio show "In the Workplace" is a popular forum for discussing current workplace issues. He is credited with creating the genre of "business bullet" books and is a regular commentator on major media forums.

CPSIA information can be obtained at www.ICGtesting.com
Printed in the USA
LVOW12s1230230714

395547LV00001BA/1/P